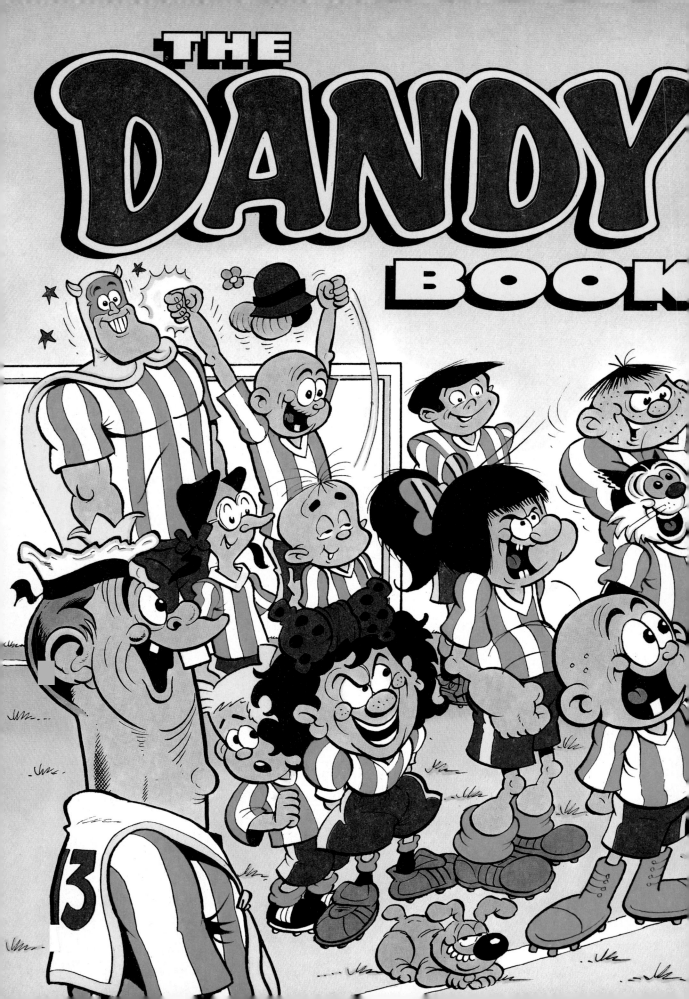

THE DANDY BOOK

GROWING PAYNES

Part two of this tale is up ahead, readers.

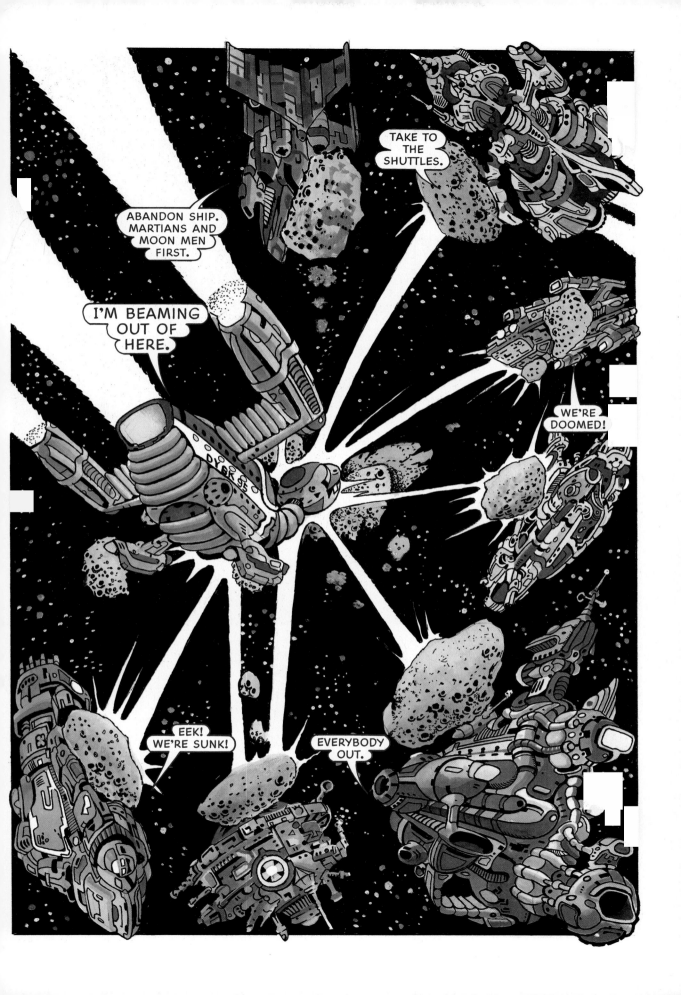

DESPERATE DAN

OLIVER TWISTER

YIPPEE! IT'S BEEN SNOWING. NOW FOR SOME FUN.

CACKLE! SNOW MEANS EVIL DEEDS. THAT'S WHAT I CALL FUN.

PLOP!

WHAT I NEED IS A CRAFTY DISGUISE.

BLOOPH!

UGH! AND NOW I'VE GOT ONE.

NOW I JUST WAIT FOR SOME RICH PICKIN'S TO COME ALONG.

BY JOVE! THAT'S AN UGLY SNOWMAN, EH, TYKE?

CLEAR OFF, WRETCH.

GRR! IT'S ABOMINABLE.

I'LL HAVE THAT, KIND SIR.

SNAFFLE!

GOOD GRIEF!

Transylvania. An archaeological dig stretches on into the night.

THIS OLD CRYPT GIVES ME THE CREEPS.

YOU'RE NOT GOING TO LET THE STORIES ABOUT THIS PLACE SCARE YOU?

WELL, THE LEGEND SAYS THAT THE CASTLE'S LAST OWNER WAS A . . . A VAMPIRE!

OLD BARON WALPURGIS DIED OVER TWO HUNDRED YEARS AGO.

YOU'RE RIGHT. AND ANYWAY, NOBODY BELIEVES IN VAMPIRES THESE DAYS.

HEY! WHAT HAPPENED TO THE LIGHTS?

IT'S PROBABLY JUST A POWER FAILURE.

POWER FAILURE? THEN WHAT IS THAT?

WHO DARES TO DISTURB THE SLEEP OF BARON WALPURGIS?

IT'S HIM! IT'S THE VAMPIRE!

RUN!

GO! OR FACE THE WRATH OF BARON BLOOD!

The next day, at the dig headquarters —

I CAN'T BELIEVE IT! OF ALL THE SUPERSTITIOUS RUBBISH!

I'M SORRY, PROFESSOR DEWARS, BUT THE WORKERS ARE SCARED STIFF. THEY REFUSE TO SET FOOT IN THE CASTLE!

BUT THE DIG MUST CONTINUE! WE'RE SO CLOSE!

DAD, CALM DOWN. THERE'S NOTHING YOU CAN DO ABOUT THESE OLD SUPERSTITIONS.

MAYBE I CAN'T, LUCY. BUT I KNOW SOMEONE WHO CAN.

IS THAT WHO YOU'RE GOING TO CALL?

YES. PROFESSOR COTFORD IS AN OLD FRIEND OF MINE. HE'S ALSO AN EXPERT ON SUPERSTITIONS AND THE SUPERNATURAL.

I'LL PROVE TO THEM THAT THERE'S NO SUCH THING AS A VAMPIRE. THEN WE CAN GET BACK TO WORK.

SORRY. I WAS LOOKING FOR MY DAD. HAVE YOU SEEN HIM?

I HAVEN'T SEEN A SINGLE SOUL. I'VE ONLY JUST ARRIVED.

OF COURSE! HE'S THE PROFESSOR.

YOU'RE THE VAMPIRE EXPERT, AREN'T YOU?

NOT AN EXPERT, NO. BUT I DO KNOW OF SUCH THINGS. ARE YOU HAVING PROBLEMS WITH VAMPIRES?

Lucy explains and —

SO, THE SCIENTISTS REFUSE TO DIG BECAUSE THEY ARE AFRAID OF THIS SO-CALLED VAMPIRE?

YOU MEAN YOU DON'T BELIEVE IN BARON WALPURGIS?

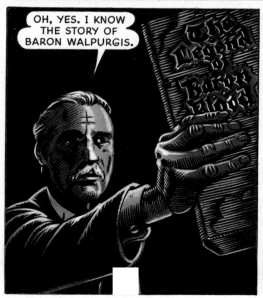

OH, YES. I KNOW THE STORY OF BARON WALPURGIS.

THE BARON LIVED AND DIED IN THIS CASTLE, TWO CENTURIES BEFORE YOU WERE BORN.

HE WAS A CRUEL AND WICKED MAN. HE LIKED NOTHING BETTER THAN TO TERRORISE THE VILLAGERS.

SO CRUEL WAS HE THAT, WHEN HE DIED, HE WAS CURSED TO ROAM THE EARTH... AS A VAMPIRE.

AND HE BECAME KNOWN IN LOCAL LEGENDS AS BARON BLOOD!

AND HE'S STILL TERRORISING PEOPLE?

IF IT IS REALLY HIM.

BUT, AFTER ALL THESE YEARS, THE BARON WOULD BE TIRED OF FRIGHTENING PEOPLE.

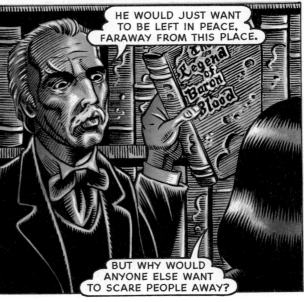

HE WOULD JUST WANT TO BE LEFT IN PEACE, FARAWAY FROM THIS PLACE.

The Legend of Baron Blood

BUT WHY WOULD ANYONE ELSE WANT TO SCARE PEOPLE AWAY?

PERHAPS THERE IS SOMETHING THEY DON'T WANT ANYONE TO FIND.

LIKE THE LOST TREASURE! THAT'S IT!

YES, THE BARON WAS SUPPOSED TO HAVE HIDDEN HIS GOLD IN THE CASTLE.

THAT'S WHAT DAD AND HIS TEAM ARE LOOKING FOR. SOMEBODY ELSE MUST WANT IT.

YOU SEEM TO HAVE SOLVED THE MYSTERY, LUCY. YOU SHOULD TELL YOUR FATHER.

DAD? I'D NEARLY FORGOTTEN.

At that moment, in the hills below the castle —

GET A MOVE ON, YOU GUYS.

FINDING THESE CAVES WAS A GREAT BIT OF LUCK. NOW WE CAN SLIP IN WITHOUT BEING SEEN.

AND THOSE BOFFINS REALLY BELIEVE OLD BARON BLOOD'S AT WORK.

YEAH. THANKS TO OUR BRILLIANT VAMPIRE DISGUISE, THE TREASURE WILL BE OURS!

Meanwhile —

DAD! OW! WHAT'S THIS?

THE PROFESSOR WAS RIGHT. SOMEONE IS TRYING TO SCARE EVERYONE AWAY.

I'D BETTER . . . HEY!!

SSSSSSH . . . LOOK!

YOU'D BETTER GET INTO COSTUME IN CASE ANYONE COMES BACK.

DON'T WORRY. WE'LL KEEP THEM SCARED AWAY UNTIL WE FIND THAT GOLD.

WE'VE GOT TO GET THE POLICE, PROFESSOR . . . PROFESSOR?

But, before Lucy has time to look for the Professor, the crook returns and —

WHO'S THAT?

YOU DARE TO TRESPASS IN THE DOMAIN OF BARON BLOOD?

THE NIGHT IS MY DOMAIN . . .

. . . AND IT IS YOU WHO IS TRESPASSING!

WHAT? WHO ARE YOU?

THE MAN YOU ARE IMPERSONATING. THE REAL BARON WALPURGIS!

WHAT WAS THAT?

And —

HELP US! IT'S THE VAMPIRE!

I THINK WE'VE FOUND YOUR PROBLEM, DEWARS.

THAT GIRL! SHE WAS WITH THE BARON!

LUCY? WHAT'S GOING ON HERE?

THEY'RE CON-MEN . . . AND PROFESSOR COTFORD DRESSED UP AS THE VAMPIRE TO SCARE THEM.

PROFESSOR COTFORD? I THINK YOU'VE MADE A MISTAKE, MY DEAR.

YOU SEE, I'M PROFESSOR COTFORD.

THEN WHO WAS THAT MAN?

HE WAS HERE! HE . . . WAIT!

The End.

CRUMP!

Fiddle O' Diddle

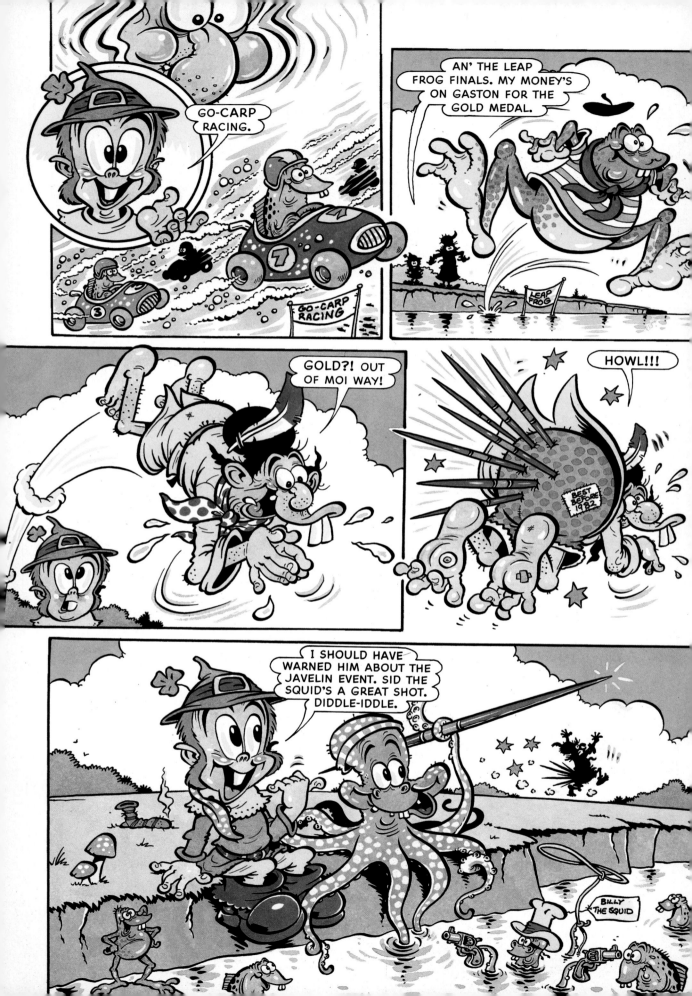

Back home —

SCOOP!

SO FAR SO GOOD.

THAT'S THE DIFFICULT BIT DONE.

PAT! PAT!

At Fred's Furniture Shop —

BED DEPT.

NOBODY ABOUT?

£250.00

£200.

£300.

I.O.U. Some
bed springs
— Beryl

GOOD.

*Back home
again —*

IN THEY GO.

Then —

SWOP, HORSE —
HAVE AN APPLE
PIE INSTEAD.

GULP!

IT'S GRIME TIME

with DESPERATE DAN

AARGH! A BULL.

Grapes — £20
2 tins beans — £5
2 togas — £65
Total £90

THE ANIMAL WASN'T MEANT TO BE WEARING ITS SKIN.

Later —

I'VE DISCOVERED THIS STUFF CALLED PAPER!

WHAT USE DOES IT HAVE?

WELL, I CAN THINK OF ONE USE.

HM! I COULD HAVE FUN WITH THAT.

LOO

But then —

THIS'LL BE USEFUL FOR WRITING ON.

ST. FRED'S

RCC

And so, the monks were able to write books.

LET'S SEE WHAT'S ON TELLY, TONIGHT.

OH, NO! TURN THAT RUBBISH OFF.

YE CORONATION STREET.

DAA-DA-DAD-DADDA-DA!

BAH!

I KNOW! I'LL GO TO THE MONASTERY AND GET A BOOK.

A BOOK? WOW!

I HOPE THEY'VE GOT SOMETHING EXCITING.

BOB'S MONK HOU

ST. FREDS

Inside, the monks are hard at work.

HAVEN'T YOU FINISHED THAT PAGE YET? YOU'VE BEEN AT IT FOR MONTHS.

I'VE ONLY GOT TWO HANDS. I'M GOING AS FAST AS I CAN.

HELLO, FOLKS. GOT ANY . . . OOPS!

YIKES!

GRR! A YEAR'S WORK RUINED.

OO-ER! KEEP CALM, MR MONK.

DESPERATE DAN at WIMBLE-DAN

Is Dan posing for a photo?

Having his portrait painted?

Getting a statue made?

NOPE! JUST UMPIRIN' THE CACTUSVILLE TENNIS FINAL. HAW-HAW!

GROWING PAYNES

IF YOU'VE SPOTTED 15 YOU'VE DONE WELL. IF YOU'VE SPOTTED 20
YOU'VE DONE VERY WELL. IF YOU'VE SPOTTED MORE THAN 20
YOU'RE A BIG FIBBER. HA! HA!

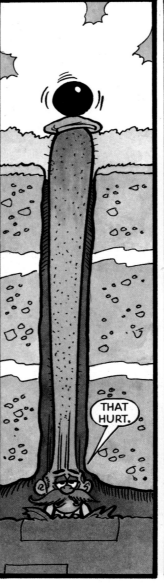

OLIVER TWISTER

MY UNCLE SILAS IS THIS SHIP'S CAPTAIN AND HE'S TAKING US ON ITS FINAL VOYAGE.

WELCOME ABOARD, YOUNG OLIVER.

BET...

CACKLE! THIS IS THE WAY US RATS BOARD A SHIP.

Out at sea —

SCRUB 'EM DECKS, BOY. I'M BO'SUN OF THIS 'ERE SHIP.

YEOW!

STORM APPROACHIN'!

THIS GIVES ME A BRAINWAVE FOR A TWIST.

I'M STORMING THROUGH MY TASK NOW, FOLKS.

RETCH!

WOOPS!

MM! A BARREL OF APPLES!

After the storm —

TONIGHT, MY PIRATE RATS, WE TAKE OVER THIS SHIP AND SAIL THE SPANISH MAIN.

THAT VOICE! IT'S FAGIN!

Later —

W-WOW! LOTS OF SHIPS ON THE HORIZON.

MERCHANT SHIPS, I'LL WAGER. LOTS OF LOOT FOR THE TAKIN'.

INTO THE BOAT, DOGS. THIS IS NOW LONG JOHN FAGIN'S SHIP.

OLD FOOL. I'D HAVE GIVEN HIM THE OLD TUB FOR FREE.

UNCLE'S SHIP WAS HEADING FOR THE SCRAPYARD AND NOW FAGIN'S HEADING FOR DISASTER.

CUDDLES AND DIMPLES

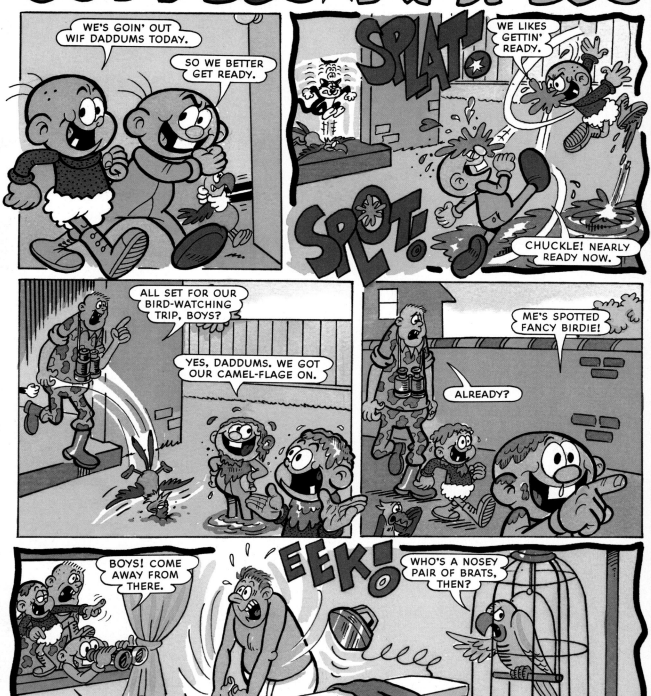

Winker Watson

LOOK AT THIS. THERE'S NOT ENOUGH HERE TO FEED A GERBIL ON A DIET.

SANDY'S RIGHT. WE NEED SOME PROPER NOSH BEFORE WE WASTE AWAY TO SHADOWS.

HMM . . . THAT GIVES ME AN IDEA FOR A WANGLE . . .

All that day —

YOUR SON PLAYED HIS PIPES AND THE ENTIRE BRITISH RAIL NETWORK STOPPED WORKING.

I KNOW HOW IT FEELS. EVERYTHING IN THE HOUSE HAS STOPPED WORKING TOO.

MOTHER, MY NEW PIPES WORK IN REVERSE. THEY STOP THINGS WORKING.

PLAY YOUR OLD ONES AND REPAIR EVERYTHING. THEY'RE IN THE BIN.

DISASTER! THE BIN HAS BEEN EMPTIED.

STOP! COME BACK!

IT'S GRIME TIME

with GROWING PAYNES

WHERE ARE YOU GOING, PERCY? IT'S TRIFLE FOR PUDDING.

IMAGINE FORGETTING MY PUDDING — WHAT A SILLY-BILLY.

SPLUT!

WELL, MUM ALWAYS SAYS I'M SWEET ENOUGH TO EAT.

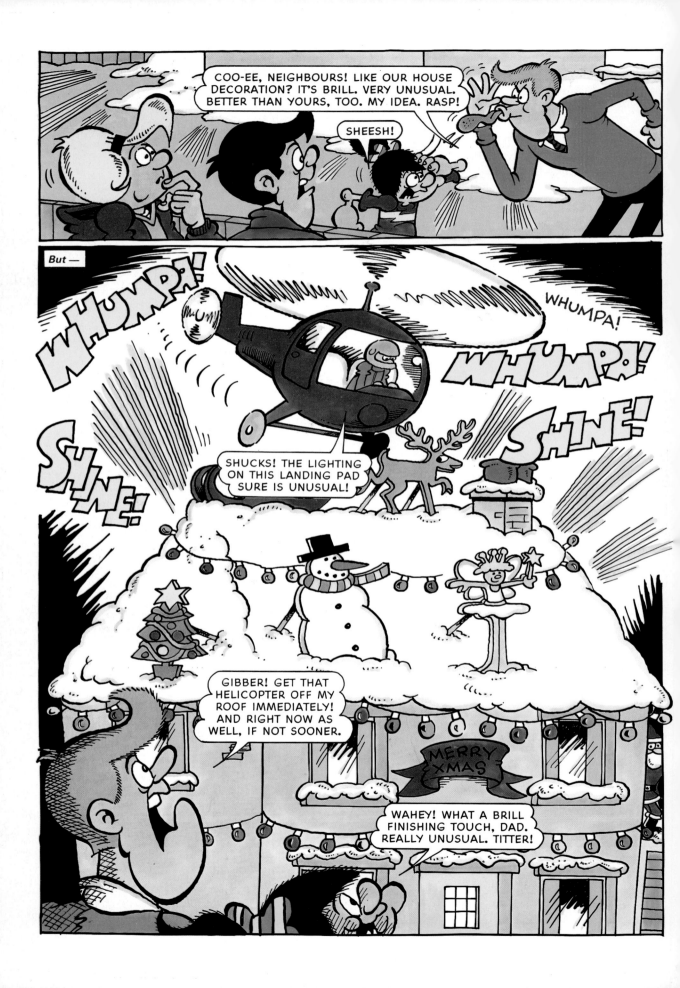

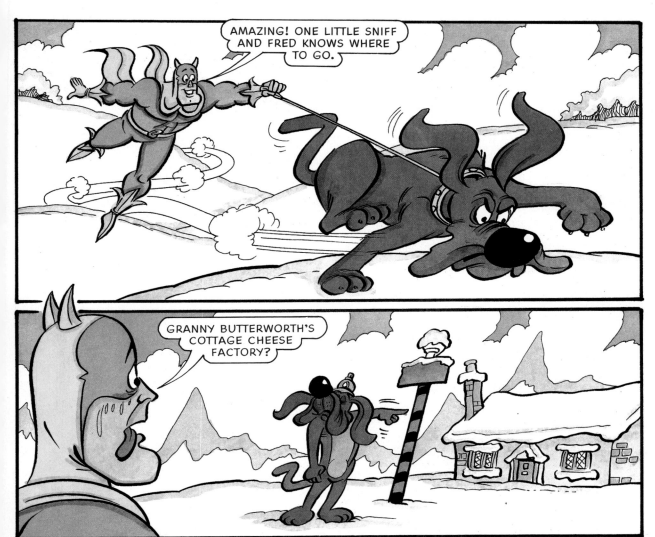